Singles' Ministry with Vision and Purpose

Virginia Freelon

www.weareaps.com

Copyright © 2015 by Virginia Freelon

All rights reserved.

No portion of this book may be reproduced mechanically, electronically, or by any other means, including photocopying, without written permission of the publisher.

ISBN: 978-1-945145-12-4

Acknowledgements

I would like to acknowledge the following individuals; without whom I may not have been able to complete this journey:

My daughter, Sanequa Natasha Young, my grandson, Thomas Antonio Young, and my granddaughter, Kaylei Tiara Young for their love, patience and understanding; for being there for me, and encouraging me throughout this entire process.

My sister, Elder Elaine Gardner, who has been inspirational.

Michele McSwain, who encouraged me to write my story.

Julie Haran-King, who has served as an inspiration in my life.

And to all of those who prophesied and encouraged me to believe in myself and persevere in realizing my dreams.

Table of Contents

Prologue............................…...1

I'm Single – Now What?........4

Keeping Intruders Out……...17

At the Conference Table..............................…...27

Revving the Next Generation......................40

Equipping Singles for Leadership.......................48

Singles Mastering Leadership……………………..53

A Heart for Singles' Ministry………………………..57

Singles Tapping into Ministry………………………72

Prologue

Being raised in church, we're taught that getting married is the right thing to do because that's how you stay in the will of God.

Having been married twice, I understand thinking that it was the right thing to do.

However, some individuals may find themselves without mates, and they need to know that there is still a place for them in ministry.

I've noticed that many churches I've attended don't even have a Singles' Ministry; it was this discovery that inspired me to write this book. I believe Habakkuk 2:2, where it advises to "Write the vision and make it plain".

My belief is that this book will help single men and women in the ministry. My intent is to help encourage and educate those who do not currently have mates, but wish to do God's will.

There will be detailed guidance of how to lead a spirit-filled discussion, a meeting of the minds among brothers and sisters in Christ.

This book is designed to teach how to establish a foundational relationship with God first, so that if and when we are joined with a "Ruth" or "Boaz", we will be ready to receive them.

Chapter 1
I'm Single – Now What?

A concern for Singles' Ministry has been addressed by several singles in the body of Christ and the church at large.

The vision and purpose of singles in ministry would be to join single men and women together as one to worship with one accord.

To create a bond that would

reach the core of their heart's desire of what single Christians are seeking inside the ministry as well as the church.

To address the needs, they have to help them grow stronger with one another without the weight of dating and seeking to be married.

Single men and women need to focus more on becoming effective leaders within the body of Christ and in the church at large.

Apostle Paul speaks to those who are single and unmarried. In 1 Corinthians 7:8, he states

"I say therefore to the unmarried and widows, it is good for them to abide even as I".

In other words, it is better that you remain single because you will have more time to fellowship with the Lord to consecrate yourself and to do those things that are pleasing to God rather than man.

If you look at the disciples who were handpicked and trained by Jesus, they were chosen based upon their willingness to totally surrender. Jeremiah 5:1 states that we are to "Run ye to and fro in broad places to seek honest men in the kingdom of God".

There need to be qualified singles willing to surrender completely to the Holy Spirit for the benefit of the ministry. Instead of coming to church simply to find a companion or mate, they should be seeking the will of God for their lives.

The truth is that all individuals were not called to be married. Unfortunately, some people don't see themselves capable of functioning without a mate. They don't see themselves in

leadership roles because they feel they must
spend all of their time consecrating.

While consecrating is necessary, it should be to get closer to God, not for Him to grant a spouse. As a leader, called by God, there should be a pure focus and purpose in attaining a leadership position.

If it's not, if the only reason why a leadership role is desired is so that a spouse can be obtained, then you should take a deeper look at your relationship with God.

The vision and purpose of Singles' Ministry should be to gather more single men and women together to work for the advancement of the ministry – not just to date.

If you do what God has called you to do, He will automatically order all that is to follow. As it states in Matthew 6:33, "Seek ye first the kingdom of God and His righteousness and all these things shall be added unto you".

If singles only knew the important role they played in the body of Christ, I believe they would be more interested in learning God's true perception of them. They can be used as instruments to get closer to God.

Because they don't have a mate to serve as a distraction, they can work without interruption – truly pray without ceasing (unless you happen to be a single parent, because children can also become a distraction).

Single people need to know that God sees their faithfulness and that He is aware of their natural needs. Being single does not separate them from the love of God, and they should not be looked upon differently because they are not married.

Unfortunately, there are some churches that treat unmarried people unfairly; it can be difficult to give your all if you feel like you are being judged.

However, the role for living a single life is just as important as the role for living a married life in the ministry.

If the goal is to have effective leadership, then the focus is not, or should not be relationship status, but the type of lifestyle demonstrated on a daily basis.

Everything that is done within the body of Christ, and the church at large, should be done decently and in order, and so if the desire is to bring singles together, there should still be a vision and purpose.

The vision and purpose for bringing singles together would be to help them find their purpose or place in the ministry. An effective way of making this determination is by organizing a round table discussion.

This platform would encourage individuals to speak openly and discuss issues that pertain to being single (something that perhaps married parties couldn't understand).

It would give them the opportunity to address their concerns without the fear of being judged. Many times, even in the church, if there is not a proper platform provided for expression, individuals may feel pressure; pressure to conform – in this case marry, could further become distracting to executing God's will.

Often time, if singles are seen talking to each other in church, the first impression is that they are dating or having sex. So many stigmas can be associated to singles whether or not they display related behaviors.

Having a round table discussion would give them the chance to speak about single life without criticism; it would also provide an opportunity for fellowship, and to be effectively trained for leadership roles.

If an individual's desire is ultimately marriage, this

platform would help to establish stronger relationships with a more spiritual foundation. They will be equipped with the tools necessary to be a stronger leader, which can help both in and out of the church.

This forum can help individuals focus more on spiritual conquests, and learn how to live in a way that is more pleasing to God. To determine what God's purpose is and how to fulfill said purpose. Some of the questions that can be asked to assist in this process are:

- Why am I single?
- When am I going to get married?
- How do I know if he/she is the one?
- How long should we date before discussing marriage or getting married?
- Should we live in the same house before marriage? Sleep in the same bed?

These are all questions that need to be addressed. When truthfully answered, they can help build a stronger foundation for dating and marriage.

Chapter 2
Keeping Intruders Out

Many single Christians desire to remain abstinent, but sometimes the pressure of dating and/or being in the same household may force marriage sooner than originally planned because of the associated guilt and shame. You want to avoid these intruders at all cost.

When I say intruders, I don't

solely mean people. Any list of things that serve as a distraction can be an intruder.

Intimacy before marriage (and the invasion of sexual spirits creeping in); pressure to uphold traditions of others to get married; and in some cases, even listening to married couples' advice can be considered intruders as they all cause your attention to be focused on something other than God's will for your life.

Forming a specified type of vision and purpose for singles in ministry could help avoid letting in unwanted spiritual intruders.

Another way to help singles avoid intruders is by heightening their awareness of the devices of wicked and unrighteous individuals.

They need to know that although intruders may exist in the church that the leaders are aware of them and will be there to help intercede on their behalf.

Having a spirit of discernment, and knowledge of right from wrong will also assist in keeping intruders out. I have found some sermons to be judgmental in nature.

As an example, when the topic is abstinence, I have heard preachers insinuate that individuals within the church are either fornicating or committing adultery.

When this is not the case, it can make people feel very uncomfortable and not want to come back to church at all, and therefore serves as a distraction from doing God's will.

Don't get me wrong, I'm not saying that it happens in every church, or that singles cannot be chastised or corrected if they are indulging in sinful behavior. I just believe that there is a particular way of addressing issues without causing harm to the individual or the church as a whole.

Just like when I stated that listening to the advice of married couples is a distraction, I am not referring to *every* married couple.

However, there are some husbands and wives that do not give righteous counsel – especially when they are going through problems in their relationship. Some couples may even prey on single Christians. These are the types of couples that I am encouraging you to be leery of.

So many faithful single men and women stop coming to church because some married couple has tried to be an intruder and play on their emotions.

They have been approached by someone (who belongs to someone else) to date them and even engage in a sexual relationship with them. When this happens, church no longer feels like a safe haven for singles, but more like a social club.

All of this intrusion has now become a distraction because it has causes shame to the single man or woman.

They now have to suffer with the guilt of messing around with someone's husband or wife, or at the very least the accusation of it all. This makes it difficult to want to show up for Sunday services or come out for prayer.

They have allowed an intruder to creep into their mind and tell them they are never going to get married; they have a sexual addiction; unable to abstain; or labeled as a cheater, fornicator, or adulterer.

This is the pressure that singles have to deal with because they desire to remain single while being in the church.

In general, any issues that can invade the mind of single men and women who are trying to remain in ministry are intruders and topics for discussion around the conference table.

The vision and purpose of

Singles' Ministry is multifaceted. It will keep singles who desire to work and function in the ministry focused on their calling.

It will train and equip them to become strong leaders. They would be encouraged to have meetings that would engage them to focus more on the importance of participating in prayer, fasting and other biblical principles.

The vision and purpose of Singles' Ministry will teach single men and women the principles of marriage, and how to maintain their relationship with God, by studying the word of God and praying daily and will help answer questions that you have about church, relationships, God, and all the things that you encounter on a regular basis.

Chapter 3:
At the Conference Table

The vision and purpose Singles' Ministry will address the singles that have been hurt in this season of their lives.

At the conference table, there will be discussions regarding the pain and disappointment of the broken relationships that the majority of Christian singles have already experienced in the ministry.

It will address what can be done within ministry to reach them and bring them back into the church instead of continuing to run them away from it.

Male or female ready to give up and never to return to any church ever again – especially the one in which they were hurt.

The vision and purpose Singles' Ministry will focus on how single men and women can be trained on becoming effective leaders in the ministry. There will be discussion on training the next generation as well. Propelling them to their next levels, both naturally and spiritually, will also be addressed.

Another aspect will be consecration. The Singles' Ministry will teach how to properly consecrate on marriage; how to focus on the promises and plans that God has for the couple individually and collectively.

It will cover how they can be married and still live an exceptional and pleasing life before God according to the Word of God. Other topics that are related to the vision and purpose of Singles' Ministry can also be discussed.

One of the most important elements of conducting an effective Singles' Ministry will be the ability to lead by example. The single men and women will need to be equipped and prepared for the 21st century forum that will guide them into all truth about the value of being and living single.

The table conference is not just focused on single men and women in the church. Its purpose is about reaching the next level of entry into the

Kingdom of God, instead of preaching the same type of sermons that have proven ineffective.

It is not necessary to purposely embarrass people, when God did not call us to judge. Sermons based on fornication, adultery, and homosexuality are necessary, but ranting in the pulpit with personal opinions and labeling it as the Word of God can cause more confusion and strife in the church.

Preaching should address sins as a whole – not just particular individuals, and more specifically, single men and women because there are those who are married who also commit sins and should be addressed.

The goal of Singles' Ministry would be to use appropriate means to address sins and sinners, while being mindful of the way that the message is conveyed.

Using the Word of God as it is intended will allow people to feel welcome within the church at large. Emulating God's love and compassion for people would allow them to be more open to listen to the Word.

Then they can gain an understanding of the wrong that they are committing in their own time frame and change accordingly, instead of being talked about by those in the church.

They would willingly want to come, as Jesus compels in Matthew 11:28 and 29, "Come unto me all ye that labor and are heavy laden and I will give you rest. Take my yoke upon you, and learn of me; for I am meek and lowly in heart: and ye shall find rest unto your souls".

Meeting at the conference table should be held once a month to maintain focus on the things of daily and spiritual life. It will allow participants to be accountable of their decisions as it pertains to righteous living.

It will be something that they can count on – an outlet specifically for single men and women.

Singles' Ministry with vision and purpose will have training designed for excelling in the body of Christ; to redevelop and help deliver its members from past hurt and pain that they may have experienced.

This healing will ensure that single men and women are different from within; being made whole will help them in living lives that are holy, which will in turn benefit the body of Christ.

The Singles' Ministry is not solely intended for one particular denomination. It is purposed for any church that wants to see creative change; any church who believes that God is calling for stronger leaders; any church that have single men and women, and understand the importance of meeting needs and addressing people where they are so they can help to build them and make them stronger.

The Singles' Ministry will highlight the following:
- Issues not frequently discussed in the church at large, but addressed in secular platforms (we want to provide a righteous forum to address any concern as all things are covered in the Word of God)
- The importance of abstaining from sexual relationships or relationships that can

tempt you to desire sex (especially if marriage isn't being considered). It is not okay to have a relationship outside of marriage. Sleeping with your best friend or friends with benefits is unacceptable for Christians living in the body of Christ and as born again believers.

- How to abstain; how to keep your mind focused without allowing the flesh to overtake you (1 Corinthians 7:9 states, "But if they cannot contain, let them marry:

- for it is better to marry than to burn)

These are all issues that can be discussed on a monthly basis and group feedback should be encouraged.

Suggestion boxes can also be made available for those that may have comments, ideas or questions and may not want to ask aloud.

The Singles' Ministry with vision and purpose has the potential to make great changes within the church if implemented correctly.

Single men and women can experience exponential growth – not just naturally, but spiritually, which will help the church become a better place. Prepare for a global explosion!

Chapter 4: Revving the Next Generation

In order to teach our next generation, we will have to set God at the head of the conference table.

To help guide and instruct us to train up our next generation that is coming behind us; to show them how to be single (if they so choose) in the ministry.

Preparing the next generation to become effective leaders while living single in the body of Christ and the church at large is going to take a lot of motivation.

They will look to the leaders who are now in ministry to teach them biblical statutes and principles of how to abstain from sexual activity and other sinful behaviors.

In short, they will need to learn the same value of the vision and purpose orchestrated by God.

They will form an allegiance

and bond with purpose to be aligned with the order which has been established. Due to the differences within the groups, it may be necessary to take the following actions:

A. Separate the groups
    1. Single men and women with children
    2. Single men and women without children
B. Form activities that relate to each group
    1. Finances
    2. How to relate to one another
    3. Discuss broken

relationships
   a. Parent
   b. Children
 4. Set up programs that can help restore their homes
 5. Bring families together
C. Follow up with a leadership conference for singles only starting with adults without children, then those with children.

There are three different ways in which these individuals can be addressed: single men and women; singles with children; singles without children.

The purpose for the leadership conference would be to inform them of the vision and purpose of Singles' Ministry.

It is not about finding a husband or wife; getting a date; or going out socially.

The focal point would be to teach and motivate those in attendance on the importance of a relationship with God; and to train them for leadership for the Kingdom of God and the church at large.

After leaving the conference, they should be able to function out of their gifts and callings for the fulfillment of the church. They should have a foundational understanding of values and principles of dating while living single in the Kingdom of God.

Gaining a personal relationship with God as a leader, they must be willing to act in obedience to those that have rule over them.

They should understand the overall importance of leadership, as well as their role in it. God has given us leaders to be watchmen over us. Singles in the ministry must be willing to deny themselves and obey the Holy Spirit as stated in Matthew 16:24, "If any man will come after me, let him deny himself, and take up His cross, and follow me".

Building this type of relationship will give you the true knowledge of where and why the type of singles' meeting was formed.

Balance will be one of the key topics addressed, especially for singles with children as well as how to date. Singles with or without children must first seek recognition from God rather than man.

In order to be qualified for the Kingdom of God you must be prepared for the 21st century vision and purpose in Singles' Ministry.

Chapter 5: Equipping Singles for Leadership

The next 21st century singles will not be self-indulgent. They will not be trained for puppy love relationships. They will be prepared to train the next generation to come.

The participants of the 21st century Singles' Ministry will be equipped to yield themselves under the mighty hand of God. They will be ready to be obedient and sacrifice everything for the benefit of the Kingdom.

At the conference table, attendees should be talking about building up character that will lead them into the Kingdom of God, and His plans for their marriages, and eliminate distractions that causes us to abort the plans and visions of God's given purposes.

This Singles' Ministry training is to establish and help build a strong relationship for those that are willing to see a life-long partner in marriage as well as an intimate relationship in Christ, having a balance on both worlds.

A strong relationship within the Kingdom of God and outside of marriage for those that desire to remain single and for those that desire to be in covenant relationship being married.

There are ordained spiritual leaders that have the abilities to help others in the next generation to live a stronger life being single. To live a Holy and pleasing single life in the Kingdom of God and to be fulfilled through the work of service in the ministry.

God is releasing specific gifts in the body of Christ along with new and divine order to regain the confidence in His people.

These will be gifts and talents that are going to equip them for the next level of service. According to Ephesians 4:11-12, "And He gave some apostles, and some prophets, and some evangelists, and some pastors and teachers; For the perfecting of the saints, for the work of the ministry, for the edifying of the body of Christ".

Simply put, this means to help them focus on God's purpose and plans for their lives, and to live as one in the body of Christ in order to keep the flesh under subjection; to be able to abstain and live before God until the consummation of marriage.

Chapter 6: Singles Mastering Leadership

It will be no getting around obeying the true aspiration of the vision and purpose for Singles' ministry, and God's Will and plans for your life.

As singles becoming leaders in the body of Christ, you must master your habits by disciplining yourself under the daily pressure of the attack of wicked devices.

One of the keys to mastering our habits is staying focused through meditating and studying the Word of God.

Have you ever broken yourself of a bad habit? In order to lead others, you must master yourself. It takes personal integrity and desire to break a bad habit.

It is very difficult to lead others if you cannot master yourself. As a matter of fact, there are many tragedies in the church today that gets

singles off-balance.
The body of Christ has failed to master itself, just as the secular and political world.

Paul spoke of this way clearly and precisely in the Book of 1 Timothy. He said that if a man desires the ministry of a bishop or a deacon (in other words, a leadership role), he must first master his own house.

You cannot fully conquer kingdoms until you have conquered yourself. Mastering yourself in singles ministry, will help you, as a leader, to overcome negative, violent spirits.

"Leaders should not be easily manipulated by the behavior or offenses of others."
Myles Munroe

God is not pleased with the church at large preaching one thing but doing something entirely different outside of what you are doing inside the four walls of the church.

As leaders, we must lead by example, not by mere words alone. We must combine words with action, which holds much evidence according to conduct; a life that determines your position as a leader.

Chapter 7: A Heart for Singles Ministry

As singles in the ministry, we are commanded to take on the same responsibility as our leaders, and to live under the influence of the Holy Spirit by denying the flesh daily in order to operate in complete honesty.

Today many people called to the ministry are not true and honest followers of Christ.

They never truly acknowledge their sinfulness and wrongdoing until they get caught or exposed by the media.

So many leaders are falling dead in the ministry, and the people of God are being scattered throughout other churches with no background training.

Singles for the 21st Century Leadership must confess and state, at the conference table, a great need of forgiveness. Forgiveness needs to be addressed immediately and trust given to God for complete deliverance.

The vision and purpose of this Singles' Ministry says that you must bear the noble title of living single in ministry.

Every powerful man or woman of God longs for someone they can trust to help work beside daily in fulfilling their God-given vision, purpose and plans for his or her living single in the Ministry.

An honest single man or woman in the church must lead by example. You have to bring your entire being under subjection to the mighty Hand of God – there's no getting around it!

Operating completely out of truth and honesty according to Jeremiah 5:1 and Matthew 16:24. As singles you are going to have total access to the Singles' Ministry, being led by the Holy Spirit that gives you every opportunity to yield your mind, body and soul unto obedience.

Matthew 7:17-20 paraphrased

admonishes to watch out for false prophets and false teachers. It explains that they show up in sheep's clothing, but inwardly they are ferocious wolves. It further goes on to say that by their fruit you will recognize them.

Singles, be reminded that you are being equipped to lead, not date. The vision and purpose of Singles' Ministry has nothing to do with the Dating Game.

Sitting at the conference table brings guidance to your inner man, and will train you to gain the sole purpose of God's plan in your single life.

Becoming an effective single in ministry as well as in the body of Christ, you will be trained to function, operate and control your flesh. Put the mindset of dating on the backburner.

There will be no more gathering up in the church to find a husband or wife. The church is not a Meet and Greet, or place for dating.

Enough with turning the church into a club! The church is a house of prayer, where we come to worship and lift up holy hands unto the Lord.

The Lord has a heart for the singles. For it is written, (paraphrasing) The Singles careth for the things of the world because it is your husband, man and wife. It was created for marriage. He has not forgotten about the single men and women.

He desires strong relationships in marriage. Adam and Eve did not date; they were consummated immediately unto marriage, without sexual intercourse first.

At the conference table, these

are the topics that will be discussed. How to complete, conclude and finish what you started in your relationship; no more broken marriages.

Marriages are supposed to be forever and should be achieved and accomplished to endure longevity once we gain each other's trust. Stay focused on what is needed to get singles prepared for their marriage.

Do not lose sight of your true purpose in this next forum. Sitting at the conference table for Singles' Ministry to gain and establish a personal, one-on-one relationship before marriage.

Remember, some of you are going into relationships with children, coming out of broken relationships, divorce and trying to find another man or woman with whom you can consummate.

The definition of consummation is "To make a marriage complete by having sexual intercourse", not dating, or going from this person to that person, in and out of different peoples' lives. A relationship that will complete each other forever.

True singles in ministry, practice love instead of teaching tradition and commands of men's doctrines. You need to get to know him, stay with him, be single for a while and find out if you like him or her sexually before you get married.

The devil has been destroying relationships much too long; it is time to boot him out.

This meeting with singles at the conference table is bringing on a different approach. Singles will gain a larger impact about living single inside as well as outside the four walls.

The vision and purpose of Singles' Ministry is going to be global, training up singles in ministry to take up their cross and break off the soul ties that have been holding them bound.

The new generation of singles living in the church or outside the Church will live their lives based on doctrine orchestrated in God's Word, the Bible.

They are not easily persuaded by the doctrine of man and the world's way of living. They are not divided by race or culture and displayed by false love amongst themselves.

Singles at the conference table will be true and honest leaders upholding high moral standards that qualify them to train and develop good fruit from those that they place into positions of authority and self-control.

They will prepare singles in ministry to equip and train others for the next level.

Singles that have a purpose for his or her ministry aggressively search out others who are just as aggressive, energized and diligent to be a part of the 21st Century Singles in Ministry.

In the process of training up effective singles in ministry, one must be very selective.

It is going to be very imperative that when choosing or training singles coming in after your completion of training that one must be very careful who they allow in the circle.

Be ye ever watchful and scrutinizing of everyone that comes in. Because of the vision and purpose, singles in ministry has gone global.

Singles are going to be hungry for this new type of ministry. They will come from the east, south, north and west in that order, thirsty for a new outlook in Singles in the Ministry-type forums.

A new avenue for singles in ministry and living single inside the body of Christ and the church at large has taken on a new approach.

It is not about dating, it's about consummation and marriage. Be alert at all times, remain watchful of the different characteristics of a person. Listen to what they say as well as the tone of the speaking that comes from their mouth.

Singles that are being equipped and trained in the ministry must be able to discern a false teacher and prophet speaking over their lives.

Chapter 8: Tapping into Ministry

Singles in ministry cannot be annoyed by people. Future singles must learn that they will be challenged by others, both in and outside of the ministry.

Singles must focus on their inner potential, and consider the behavior of their character. Singles' Ministry separates a person's behavior from their self-worth and does not confuse their value with their condition.

Being in Singles' Ministry in the Kingdom of God, you must be a person who knows how to deal effectively with your future as well as the future of others.

Encourage other singles to train others, and to lead by example. Then you can see the fruit of your work performed in the 21st Century Singles' Ministry.

True followers of Christ will

shew forth in other true followers. A single in ministry is one who is willing to take up their cross and carry it for the sake of its followers as examples. It shows others how to live as singles in and out of the church at large.

How long should you court in a relationship before marriage? First, define courting, preparation for marriage. Some say six months at the most, or 2 years, if you can withstand the pressure of abstaining from intercourse.

There's no girlfriend or boyfriend going on; you are

getting to know him or her by kissing or grinding to see how it will or IF it will spark a fire.

And, if not that, how will you know you are ready to be as one, or even as God ordained man and woman to live in matrimony unto Him; to live a Holy and pleasing life with Him.

If you already experienced how each other looks or feels, possibly having orgasms with all the petting and embracing, this is the subtle works of the devil telling you that it is okay; there's nothing wrong with getting familiar with one another before marriage.

Since we are in the process of making a commitment to one another, you won't surely die?

God understands that we are all adults and that we know we have fleshly needs, or He wouldn't have created us that way.

That's why He encourages us to wait, so we can experience the meaning of 'until death do us part' as what everlasting love would be like, love that will never fail.

This is why Singles' with a

vision and purpose in Ministry will share a greater outlook on dating in churches.

It will change how we approach each other, looking at each other with respect and not lust. Deciding that we need each other as business partners and as friends.

Building up the Kingdom of God to fulfill our vision and purpose in Singles' Ministry without the dating.

Building relationships to further our reason for being single and our purpose to become as one in being married according to God's Plan.

Wait and be still to see what direction God leads you. Listen to the voice of God, what God is really saying to the single men and women out there.

There is a vision and purpose in Singles' Ministry for the 21st Century that can change the nation for single men and women that want to be married or just remain single and live a life without fornication.

By seeking the Face of God for

the right person that has the same heart for you and God.

It is to make sure they have a heart after God, to live in total honesty, trust and love for each other. So, those are the things that can be generated throughout the relationship.

To be sold out together having the same mindset. Both single men and women will be sold out, pursuing the same purpose and vision in the relationship.

Striving to seek out that someone that you can confide in and have that relationship without the game of pretense, testing the waters over and over again, finally finding the one that you can trust and be honest with.

Why Am I Still Single?

Refusing to change, holding on to old habits and continuing to fall short of what they deserve.

Choosing to settle without knowing their self-worth, or self-value, giving in because of life's pressures from others, and not waiting to listen for the real person their heart is speaking of.

"Someone mature enough to understand that loyalty, commitment and honesty is a priority and not an option".
EyeOpenerQuotes.com

Settling is not an option, so where did you get off track? Did you follow the guidelines in front of you? Or did you put it back on top of the bookshelf?

This book gives simple steps one, two and three. It starts out by keeping you away from the intruders through tapping into ministry.

Steps four through seven keeps

you from yourself by keeping your flesh under subjection.

Let's start by looking into the mirror after steps one, two and three, not pointing fingers at each other, but examining yourself in the mirror. Before you strip yourself by taking your clothes off and letting someone else expose you, expose yourself.

I am being purged for this person's husband or this person's wife. He or she will be better off with me. Go over the book again, living as a single, and this time, don't leave out God.

www.ingramcontent.com/pod-product-compliance
Lightning Source LLC
LaVergne TN
LVHW051849080426
835512LV00018B/3150